Champagne Pain

Sheree' Morris

A collection of poems about finding peace during life's storms of turbulent emotions, setbacks, and disappointments.

Copyright©2017 Sheree' Morris

All rights reserved

Willie & Willie Publishing Inc.

ISBN: 0692045295

ISBN-13: 978-0692045299

Persistence Breathes Life into Dreams®

Expectations (Author's Note to Reader)

    To all those who manage to find this book

please take the time to give this a look

please don't give up on the things you dream

no matter how far away they seem

    Don't let go of what you believe

you're not the only one who believes in impossibility

sometimes you feel like you've reached the brink...

and you'll never see the things you think

    Doesn't matter what the cause of your passion

just don't give up on the chance to imagine

I hope you understand all the words I say

though they're stated in a different way

Maybe it's been long and maybe you're tired
but please don't give up on what you aspire
maybe you have something to say
or you're waiting on someone who'll listen
whatever the case, continue to go the distance

    If you give up now, what else will you choose? maybe you've something this world can't afford to lose

maybe you think you're too young or even too old
all I know, is your story deserves to be told

    So, if you wake up to another day of lack,
and it makes you rethink what you ask...
don't give up, please understand
very seldom, are you the only one affected by your plan

    If you watch what you imagine, manifest in someone else

let's be honest, you'll never forgive yourself

I know expectations can sometimes be labored meditations

but you've got to pursue the revelation

    If you don't have what you want, please continue to wait

please don't settle; it's never too late

please don't give up; don't let go

I want you to know, you're never alone

    Continue to exist, continue to persist

continue to expect the hopes you believe

whatever you do...

Don't walk away from your dreams!

Contents

Chapter 1: Sober

Learning Curve 2

Precious Gift 4

Intentions 5

How do you Cope 6

Chapter 2: Buzzed

Tipsy 10

Emotional State 12

Sheer Will 14

Silence 15

Chapter 3: Inebriated

To the Unknown 18

Ode to Peace 19

Open Wound 20

Champagne Pain 22

Chapter 1

Sober

Learning Curve

Life will bring all the lessons you deserve

knowledge can come at a hefty price

take your time, don't hasten the curve

There's wisdom in those who consider and observe

than those who hasten to the will of bad advice

life will bring all the lessons you deserve

Love will either strengthen your resolve or break your nerve

shapely lips can often quicken and entice

take your time, don't hasten the curve

Put all experience in a treasured reserve

innocence will soon be a lost paradise

life will bring all the lessons you deserve

Hold onto youth as much can be preserved

age comes with much sacrifice

take your time, don't hasten the curve

When enlightenment seems on delay

don't fret you'll know all one day

life will bring all the lessons you deserve

Take your time, don't hasten the curve

Precious Gift

It is the present that cannot be left behind

the truth that every man must find

the gift that all must treasure

the gift that gives life pleasure

When vanity ceases to entertain

your presence will still remain

imploring everyone to believe

in the power of your abilities

The power to make division pale

in a heart that's grown stale

the power to ease the strain

on a heart weakened from pain

The power to give hope for tomorrow

from a past filled with sorrow

it is the present we all dream of…

It is the gift of love

Intentions

Have the intention to change the mold

Get out of line and take your place

Break the chains that have a hold

Don't be afraid to show your face

There's nothing more engaging

than to discover your truth

See your world in a new way

Find the parts of you, you never knew

See yourself differently than you did yesterday

Have every intention to be free

Find the courage it takes to live bold

Whether or not others like what they see

Free your eyes from the blindfold

Let your personality consume every day you wake

Then you'll have no room to be fake

How do you cope?

How do you cope?

they always say,

when something else goes astray.

What's next?

they always ask,

when what you want has passed.

What do you do, when everyone gets awarded but you?

when you've done more than anyone can mention,

but you still can't get recognition.

I don't get it?

you've plenty understanding for any mate

but you can't find anyone to relate.

They ponder...

maybe you've already held the hand of whom you desire?

but you know what your heart requires.

They say,

you have admirers you ignore

but you know they're not the one you're waiting for.

They ask,

How do you cope?

Sometimes I don't know...

I just have hope.

Chapter 2
Buzzed

Tipsy

Pardon me if I stutter

But I'm all a flutter

It's a little hard for me to explain

There's confusion in my brain

My heart beats amiss

From the fragrance of your scent

And the tenderness of your kiss…

Is a lingering torment

Onlookers may think

I've had too much to drink

But how can I make them believe

Your presence makes me weak at the knees

The passion you control

Touches me to my soul

My composure falls apart

When you connect with my heart

It's not the wine that makes me stumble

To your will I am humble

My heart leaps and skips a beat

When you're standing here next to me

How can I help but be

A little tipsy

Emotional State

Man, I'm in an emotional state

Every time I breathe I ache

Every time I think I break

Every time I move I shake

Every time I breathe I ache

I wake with a heart full of pain

Every time I move I shake

I open my eyes with weary disdain

I wake with a heart full of pain

My heart feels like it was put in upside down

I open my eyes with weary disdain

My shoulders feel like they weigh a thousand pounds

My heart feels like it was put in upside down

I dress my body with unrelenting sorrow

My shoulders feel like they weigh a thousand pounds

I pray for a better demeanor tomorrow

I dress my body with unrelenting sorrow

It makes me want to kneel and weep

I pray for a better demeanor tomorrow

Why does the feeling go so deep

It makes me want to kneel and weep

All of the world's emotions gather at this place

Why does the feeling go so deep

You can see the burden all over my face

All of the world's emotions gather at this place

It's like I'm sinking into a black hole

You can see the burden all over my face

It goes all the way down to the depths of my soul

It's like I'm sinking into a black hole

Guess I'm left alone to battle this spirit

It goes all the way down to the depths of my soul

Spew it out, fight, and choke it

Guess I'm left alone to battle this spirit

It's just one day, it's not my fate

Spew it out, fight, and choke it

Man, I'm in an emotional state

Sheer Will

When the end of destination

Is left in the hands of determination

When theology no longer boast

And humanity has given up the ghost

When pride no longer has a space

And six feet of reality is the only place

When I've reached beyond what I know

And the only thing left is a yes or no

When all those who care have wept

And what was acquired can no longer be kept

When the only question is if I'll linger still

May I find faith in sheer will

Silence

Don't move a muscle don't say a word

Let the silence be the only thing that's heard

Just let me think just let me breathe

Right now there's no other place to be

Here I am still I don't have to shelter what I feel

The silence is the only thing that's real

As I pursue with all persistence

To understand the truth of my existence

In the silence I can release no one is here judging me

I can take a step and no one would know

No one to tell me how far I can go

The silence allows me to wonder beyond what I can see

And no one here to ask what's bothering me

The silence just listens until my lamenting ends

And waits patiently like a faithful friend

The silence embraces me and draws me near

Then leans in and whispers...

What are you doing here

Chapter 3

inebriated

To the Unknown

    You think no one can see you
That no one will understand your truth
That every glance will just be a start
To a relationship that tears apart
    That no one will be able to speak
On the knowledge that you keep
That no one will be able to compare
To the essence that you bare
    That you will not be able to find
A partner of your kind that no one will be able to understand all the callouses on your hand
    You don't have to sacrifice the rareness of your creed, to reap the benefits of your seed
Someone holds the key to the question of your mystery and once the truth is shown
Your heart will never be unknown

Ode to Peace

You are the balm for a wound that's been opened

And the solace for the broken

The resolution that every scar bought

The longing sigh every empty heart wrought

You are the destination finally reached

The last word of every speech

The final breath of a life's worth of days

The very reason for one last special ordered bouquet

The welcomed reward of choices well spent

The very dream of a hopeful ascent

The assurance to those who cry

Over precious flowers that wither and die

When expectations have finally grown tired and weak

You are exhilaration at its peak

When truth is discovered from what was preached

And raging storms and howling cease

There is finally peace

Open Wound

There once was a girl who had a large cut on her breast

Sometimes it would hurt deep down in her chest

The cut caused her a lot of pain

And she didn't know if she'd ever be the same

It dictated everything she could be

And clouded everything she could see

She spent every day with her shoulders burdened low

And a heart full of woe

She didn't know if she'd ever see

An end to her misery

Then one day she took a chance on a precarious deed

And the cut began to bleed

She gathered many bandages in her hand

And tied them into a band

She continued to perform so her friends wouldn't know

She pasted on a smile so the pain wouldn't show

No matter if she was happy or not

She couldn't make the wound clot

So she decided to leave the wound alone

Maybe it would heal on its own

She shrugged her shoulders and decided to ignore

All the pain she had stored up before

Since she couldn't keep the pain at bay

She decided to live her life anyway

She took a chance on an understanding hand

And before she knew it she was able to stand

Slowly she began to feel

That the wound began to heal

Then one day when they were walking along

She noticed that the pain was gone

The wound that had threatened to bury her in decay

Had finally gone away

Champagne Pain

Pour me another glass of champagne

I need a break from the pain

Sometimes the tingling is so strong

I've been drinking it for so long

    I take a sip, then I savor

I taste the hints of every flavor

I know the notes of every scent

It's filled the air of every day I've spent

    Sometimes it leaves my mouth feeling dry

But it moistens when I cry

Sometimes when it's a bit crisper

It reduces my moans to a whisper

    Sometimes the aroma is a pleasant bouquet
And it hides the scars of dismay
When there's a fruitiness in the smell
Then I know, I'm under its spell
    Give me a full-bodied kind of wine
That's how I'll take it every time
Sometimes I taste a sweetness in the finish
And I grimace
At the desire of the glass to be replenished
    So, pour me another glass of champagne
As I make a toast to the pain.

www.ingramcontent.com/pod-product-compliance
Lightning Source LLC
Chambersburg PA
CBHW032101150426
43194CB00006B/604